ALL THINGS GIRL

Friends, Boys, and Getting Along

TERESA TOMEO
MOLLY MILLER
MONICA COPS

© 2008 by Teresa Tomeo, Molly Miller, and Monica Cops

Published by
Bezalel Books
Waterford, MI
www.BezalelBooks.com

Other titles in the ALL THINGS GIRL series:
Mirror, Mirror on the Wall…What is Beauty After All?
Girls Rock!
Mind Your Manners
Modern and Modest

Printed in the United States of America

ISBN 978-0-9818854-1-4
Library of Congress Control Number 2008931733

THIS BOOK IS DEDICATED TO...

"To my Grand Niece Julianna.
Welcome to the world. Remember you are a daughter of the King. I love you."
Aunt Tree

"To my Lucy, who has been my inspiration for All Things Girl."
Love, mom

"To the most beautiful Princesses in my life, Elena and Adriana"
Love, mom

High Class

All people begin life in their mother's womb. Ever since God created you, a tiny little creature, you were already a person! Being created a person is different from any living things because God gave you a soul that will live forever. He loves the cats and dogs He created, but they only have bodies. A person is a creature composed of body and soul. Being a person, you are in a higher class because your soul is what gives you the image and likeness of God. Your creator, God the Father, has stamped dignity in your soul. What is dignity? It is your worth as a person. It is something that can't and doesn't go away. Not for any reason. Dignity is a beautiful gift that God has given you.

Dignity has three characteristics:

It is not dependent on any circumstances within which you live.

It doesn't matter what you look like.

It does not change, even when you do.

Jennifer lives in a neighborhood where the houses are very small and the people work hard but don't have much money. Katie lives in a mansion and takes expensive vacations every year. Which person has more dignity?

Jade is from Africa and has deep brown skin. Julie has red hair and freckles. Laura is chubby. Maggie is tall and skinny. Which girl has more dignity?

Opal is 95 years old and lives in a nursing home. She has to be spoon-fed. Riley was in a car accident and has a huge scar on her face. Which person has more dignity?

Hopefully you answered "neither" to all of the examples because all people are equal in dignity. In your life you will go through good times and bad times, sorrows and joys, accomplishments and failures. Some people may tell you that all these things are what defines you as a person, but do not believe them, they are wrong! These things may have an impact on you but do not define you as a person.

The only thing that defines you as a person is the fact that you are a daughter of God. This is your greatness, your highest dignity.

Compared to this, what really matters? Power, money, fame or anything else you could get in this world, what is it in comparison to belonging to God's family?

At this point you should be feeling quite good about yourself. Just in case you need more, check it out, it gets better!

Princess

When you were a baby, your mom and dad brought you to Church to be baptized. What does baptism do? It washes away original sin, makes you a child of God and fills your soul with grace. God is the King of the universe, and you are His daughter: that makes you a princess! As a princess in the royal family of God, you have a value greater than a rare jewel and He loves you soooooo much.

So you see, you are so much more than body parts. You are intelligent, creative and caring. You are not an object, but a person, and a female person at that! Sexuality is what makes you a girl, different from males. Being created a girl is special. Only a woman can carry another living person within her body. God also gave to women unique gifts such as a nurturing heart, a giving spirit, and a detail oriented mind. These gifts are used for the good of those around you and for your own true happiness.

Lots of girls grow up trying to answer the soul-searching question of **"Why am I here?"** The answer is simple, *To know, love, and serve God in this life and to be happy with Him forever in Heaven in the next.* You get to *know, love and serve God from Jesus Christ, the Son of God, who teaches us through the Catholic Church.* (Baltimore Catechism)

But how do you do all these? Let's take it by steps:

1. To know God:

What would you do if you wanted to get to know a movie star? You'd try to read up all the information about him or her in magazines and books, you would watch interviews on television, and ask people around you what they know, about this movie star. Well, you get to know God in a similar way: reading the Bible, listening to your parents talking about God, taking your religious class seriously, praying and receiving the Sacraments.

2. To Love God:

How do you get to love a friend? Well, by spending time with her. You do things together and talk with that friend. To fall in love with God, you also need to spend time with Him in prayer and adoration, and worshipping Him at Sunday Mass. You can tell Him things and make time to listen to Him talk to you.

3. To Serve God:

You serve God by serving other people. Serving God is doing daily chores cheerfully without complaining, or participating in service projects. Jesus once said that when we take care of other people we are taking care of Him. Jesus was letting us know that He is in each of us so serving others really, truly is serving God!

Single

Wife   Religious

Mother

A word about Vocation

As you grow up, ask Our Lord how He wants you to know, love and serve Him. This will be your vocation. Vocations are the unique ways in which each person is called by God. Everyone has a special gift or talent that is given by God. You are happiest when you find out what that is and use it to serve God and His kingdom. It is fun to work with God and discover your vocation!

The Jewels in Your Crown

What would a princess be without jewels? As a daughter of the King you have jewels in a crown, but not the kind of jewels that are valuable stones. You have something way more precious! Your jewels are attributes or qualities represented by different colors. Craft idea: make a bracelet using the below colors to remind you of your attributes as the daughter of the King.

 *Color Attributes*

Yellow

Yellow represents joy. True joy is a satisfaction you feel deep inside when you really believe God loves you. A great way to experience true joy is to remember JOY-Jesus first, Others second, and You last. When you live trying to please yourself last, not insisting on getting your own way, you will be truly happy. St. Joan of Arc is a great girl saint who put God's will and her country ahead of herself. She experienced great joy even as she died a martyr. Sometimes we see when other people are thinking only of themselves but miss it in ourselves. You can avoid this when you remember what "joy" really is: Jesus first, Others second, You last.

Blue

Blue represents loyalty, which is having a bond to a person, faith, or country. This means you stand up for a friend when she is being teased. It means keeping secrets and keeping other's faults hidden. Think of St. Mary Magdalene when she was at the foot of the cross. She remained faithful to Jesus when his friends ditched him. Jesus was loyal to each of us when He accepted the cross. It may not always be easy to be loyal but it feels good in the end.

Green

Green signifies forgiveness, the ability to accept an apology and to let things go. It is wrong to hold a grudge or try to get even with someone. Forgiving is an act of mercy. The key to forgiveness is love. Not the kind of love in movies and popular songs. Real love, like Jesus shows us, total and complete giving of self to others. He told us, "Love your enemies and pray for those who persecute you." Getting to know Jesus will help you to forgive without limits. St. Patrick is an example of this type of forgiveness. After escaping those who captured him as a child, he returned to them after becoming a priest to share the Catholic faith with them. Like loyalty, forgiveness isn't always easy but feels good in the end.

Orange

Orange means compassion. This is putting yourself in another's situation. How would you feel if you were the one who didn't get an invitation to a party, or the girl whose family doesn't have a lot of money for name brand clothes, or the girl who gets teased? Blessed Mother Teresa put herself in the poor person's shoes and ended up leaving a comfortable convent to live among the poorest of the poor. By being compassionate this little nun was able to care for thousands of unwanted people who were filthy, sick, and unloved. If she could do this, you can think of the girl who has no friends and take her in. That sounds way easier than living in the ghetto and caring for the poor, don't you think?

Pink

Pink has always been the color for girls and stands for kindness. Kindness means wanting the good of everyone, even those you don't like. It is being happy for someone when they get an award or a good grade. It is letting someone else go ahead of you in line or have her way. St. Veronica is a great example of kindness. Amidst the crowd and the soldiers she wiped the face of the suffering Jesus. As a reward of this heroic kindness, He left a picture of Himself on her veil. Does kindness sometimes seem like loyalty and forgiveness? That's because it can be! It is good to do kind things even if you don't always feel like doing them because soon God will make your heart be filled with joy from your acts of kindness.

Red

Red is charity or true love. This is not the fairy tale love of the prince and princess riding off into the sunset to live happily ever after. This is the kind of love that Jesus showed all of us by dying on the cross. This is giving of yourself until you can't give anymore. Examples of this include doing your best on all your schoolwork, it means helping mom with housework when you would rather be outside with your friends, it means letting others have their way, or staying in for recess to help your teacher. This kind of love can be really hard especially when you get no instant reward. Jesus is the best example of true charity.

Purple

Purple stands for royalty, which is a special elevation. You are a member of the royal family of God. Think of kings and queens of days gone by. They were either, fair and loving to their subjects or they were selfish and greedy, lording their power over them. It is wrong to have power over others. When someone says things like, "We're all wearing yellow tomorrow... So sorry you don't have anything yellow, I guess you're out of the group," they are trying to control or have power over others and this is wrong. St. Elizabeth of Hungary used her influence as queen to feed the poor, and to build hospitals and schools for the needy. Jesus was the most royal person ever and look what He did: He washed the feet of His disciples!

White

White is purity of heart and mind. This purity means seeing things and people as God sees them. It means seeing a girl with pimples on her face and greasy hair as a beautiful princess. It also means refusing to imagine revengeful thoughts towards someone who hurt you. The best example of this purity is Our Lady. She fully and perfectly lived out God's plan for her life. Jesus said that the pure in heart will see God. This means they will see Him in heaven but also see Him in other people.

Always remember

- As a princess you want to look and act the part. This includes treating other girls as the princesses they are, too.

- All girls are daughters of the King.

- God has a special plan for each girl, even, mean ones.

- The jewels in your crown will remind you of not only your worth but how to treat others.

- You're not in this alone. God and all His saints and angels are with you!

Jewels In Your Crown Bracelet

Supplies:

Wire Cutter

Bracelet memory wire, silver or gold

Needle nose pliers

Spacer beads

One of each of the following color beads: white, blue, purple, green, yellow, pink, red, and orange.

Beads, use the following colors: white, blue, purple, green, yellow, pink, red, orange. You can use one large bead of each color or several smaller beads used in a pattern.

Decide if you want your bracelet to be one, two or three times around your wrist. Cut the wire to the size you want. Use the needle nose pliers and bend the end into a loop to keep the beads from falling off and finish the edge.

Using the spacer beads and colored beads, create a pattern and string the beads on the bracelet wire. Finish the end with the needle nose pliers.

Wear your Jewels In Your Crown Bracelet as a fashion statement and to remind you how to be a good friend. Make several and give them to your friends. Or better yet, have a beading party and do it together with your friends.

Friends Forever

You've known each other since kindergarten and have grown up together. You want to stay friends forever! How do you know if you are the type of girl that will be a friend forever, or if she will be a forever friend? You can go back to Jewels in Your Crown and remind yourself of the qualities of a good friend. If you end up having a few true friends your whole life, you will be blessed! Friends should have the same purpose in their life as you do; to know, love, and serve God and to be happy forever in heaven. If she doesn't help you to get to heaven, she's not a good friend. And always remember that the reverse is true. If you aren't helping your friends live in such a way as they will get to heaven, you aren't a true friend.

Take this quiz to see what kind of friend you are. Circle your answer or record it someplace else just so you can be honest with yourself and find areas to work on. Catholics call this an "examination of conscience."

1) When something wonderful happens to her, like an A on a test or an award, you are so happy for her. (Purity of heart, white)

Sometimes　　　　　　Always　　　　　　Never

2) If she makes you mad, you talk to her about it and forgive her without thinking of revenge or pouting. (Forgiveness, green)

Sometimes　　　　　　Always　　　　　　Never

3) When someone makes fun of her, you stand up for her even if it means you may be the next target. (Loyalty, blue)

Sometimes　　　　　　Always　　　　　　Never

4) You know you are the daughter of the King and you respect yourself and your friend by expecting the best for each other. (Royalty, purple)

Sometimes   Always   Never

5) You put her choice of things to do ahead of your own at least half the time and say prayers for her when she needs them. (Yellow, JOY)

Sometimes   Always   Never

6) You always think the best of her even if others don't. (Kindness, pink)

Sometimes   Always   Never

7) When she is having a hard time with something, you feel her pain and try to console her. (Compassion, orange)

Sometimes   Always   Never

8) You are willing to give up going to a movie you have been dying to see to be with her when her dog dies. (Charity, red)

Sometimes   Always   Never

Tally you answers and read the key below.

Mostly Never. You are the worst friend EVER!!! If you are reading this book, you can't have gotten mostly Never.

Mostly Sometimes. You are a friend who struggles with doing the right thing all the time. Welcome to the club. Most girls have things to work on. Try to pick one of your weak areas and work on that one thing, say for a month. Before you know it you will be the best friend she will ever have!

Mostly Always.   You are a treasure! You are a true friend.

Emotions

Emotions refer to your feelings. They play a big part in your relationship with others. Some emotions have a positive effect, such as happiness, wonder, acceptance, and anticipation. Others have a negative effect, such as jealousy and anger. Feelings can be described as the caboose of a train, while your head, your ability to think, is the engine. It would be impossible for the caboose to pull the entire train, just as having the emotions run your life would be an impossible way to live.

You are in charge of how you deal with your emotions. You have to take responsibility for how you choose to act **at all times**. So if you blow up at your best friend, even though she gossiped about you, you have the choice of how you react: yelling at her, or cooling off and calling her later to discuss things. During stressful situations, you may become over-emotional. The day of the big science final, it's normal to feel edgy, but you must not let the caboose run the train. Choose to keep quiet and smile when that annoying girl with the locker next to you continues to tell you about the rate grass grows.

Certain emotions can damage friendships:

Jealousy: It is okay for your friend Cami to invite Amber to her house once in a while without inviting you. Cami is still your friend, she just wants to spend time alone with Amber. You should not feel hurt. Jealousy emerges when you feel a rivalry. Learn to be happy for others. This takes work that only you can do. Every time you get that jealous feeling, stop that thought right away and instead say a short prayer like, "Jesus help me be happy." It will take some time, but you can train your mind what to think virtuously.

Overly-sensitive: A friend should help the other become a better person. When your friend notices a bad habit of yours, let's say, being disorganized or lazy with school work, don't be upset if she brings it up to you with the intention of helping you get organized. Have a positive attitude and accept your friend's help. Sometimes girls jump to conclusions. "She must be mad at me 'cause she didn't say hi to me today…" If you jump to this kind of conclusions, you can make others miserable. Train your thoughts to always think positively and think the best of others. If sometime you are in doubt, be honest and ask your friend "Hey, how come you didn't say 'hi' to me today? She probably didn't even notice that she hadn't greeted you. And if there is something you two need to talk about, true friends are able to do just that!"

Fear: Let's say one of your friends asks you to try something new, say roller blading. Right away you get nervous about things. What if you fall? What if you twist your ankle? All you can think of what could happen that would be bad. After awhile, you become a real downer to your friends. Everyone has fears, but pray to your guardian angel and to the Blessed Mother to help you cope when you get nervous. Talk to your mom about what scares you and she can help calm your fears. Sometimes fear is a good thing and keeps you safe but if it is controlling you then it isn't good and you need to rein it in.

Anger: Nobody likes a girl with anger management issues. Being angry when you don't get your way, or something disappointing happens, like losing an important soccer game, gets old to those around you. If you throw things or have temper tantrums, you'll be lucky to have even one friend. It's good to learn how to control your anger. Take a few seconds, count to ten or even twenty. Give yourself a timeout away from people if you are mad. Write in your journal to let off steam. Say a Hail Mary or two to help you.

At your age, emotions are heightened because of all your hormonal changes. If you and your mom feel you need to talk to your doctor because you've done all you can and still struggle with your emotional ups and downs, you shouldn't feel embarrassed. Going to trusted adults, even if you just want to hear words of wisdom, usually helps. They can help you understand how important nutrition and exercise is and if you need vitamins or even just some extra sleep at night. The point is, don't let your emotions be the engine!

"Girls are made of sugar and spice and all things nice," right? Well, not all the time. But as a daughter of the King, you will be expected to act the part. But that's not always the case in girl world. Did you know there's a new term counselors are using for "mean girl?" It's "relational aggression," which basically means, girls using relationships to hurt each other. That sounds awful, but you have probably experienced this in school or in your neighborhood. There are specific characters in the world of girls. I bet you know some of them.

Snooty Susie
She's the girl everyone wants to be like. She's the Queen. She is pretty, wears the best name brand clothes, and the boys all have a crush on her. She likes to be the one to tell everyone what to do, who to like, and what to wear.

Loose Lipped Lisa
She's the one you trusted with a secret and she promised never to tell a soul and the next day the whole world knows about it.

Jenedict Arnold
You and Jen had plans to go to the movies with your family. At the last minute Jen calls to tell you she can't go because her mother needs her to help with the kids. The next day you find out Jen was with the Queen. Jen lied to you.

Cruel Kelly
Kelly goes around making fun of what people wear or stealing their stuff. Everything she does is mean- spirited and all the girls are afraid of her.

Penny the Pouter
This girl has to get her way all the time. If she doesn't she's likely to give you that look, you know the one, the pouty face. Then it's the silent treatment. There's times she may not talk to you for days to punish you for not playing her favorite CD instead of yours.

Jealous Josie

Josie is fun to be around and you really like her, until you get a gift or go on vacation and she doesn't. Then, she turns green with envy. She'll make you feel guilty by saying things like "must be nice," or "you're so spoiled." She takes all the fun out of the good things that happen to you.

Oblivious Olivia

She's a great girl but doesn't have a clue about the real world. She needs help on personal hygiene, like washing her hair and taking a shower. She's just so busy playing sports she doesn't even notice her appearance.

Studious Sarah

This girl is so smart and school comes so easy for her. She doesn't care much about fashion or being up- to -date or cool. She's in her own little world.

Cute Katie

She's a nice girl and a lot of girls like Katie. She wants to be liked and have the name brand clothes but can't afford them so she does the best she can.

Pompous Polly

Everyone knows Polly. No matter what you have, do, or experience, she has, does or experiences it way better. She's the one that is always storytelling about her experiences or stuff. No one knows what is true because she always has to "one up" everyone. She definitely has some sort of "issue" with being accepted.

Emo Emily

She would dye her hair black, pierce her nose and have a tattoo if she was allowed. She talks about depressing things and is never happy. It's totally tiring to be around Emily. She takes the joy out of every good thing. She wears her hair in her face and her wardrobe consists of basic black. What a downer.

Boyish Brenda

Brenda really doesn't want to be a girl, which is really sad. She has no idea what a privilege it is to be a girl. She grew up playing with boys and has no idea how to hang around girls. She doesn't like fashion.

Why are girls mean?

Did you recognize any of the characters? Maybe even you are like one or more of them. There are many kinds of people you have to get along with throughout your life. There will always be a mean girl in the neighborhood, at work, or in school.

So why are girls mean? The simple truth is some girls want power because they are insecure. Why would a girl be insecure? Well, maybe there are problems in the family such as a divorce, or the loss of a job. Maybe the girl doesn't feel loved or appreciated. There are as many reasons as there are girls. Whatever it is, though, it makes the mean girl feel bigger or better if she has control of others. In her eyes, if she can make someone feel low, she has power. That's pretty sad, huh? Too bad she doesn't know that she's a daughter of the king along with all the other girls in God's royal family. Maybe if she knew, she would feel better about herself.

So, What's a Girl to Do?

You've had it! Susie made fun of you again today at lunch. You want this to stop but you don't know how. Here are a few suggestions:

 Repeat often: "I am the daughter of the King." It will remind you that you are royalty and have a worth so valuable that you can't measure it in money. Wear something purple to school, even if it is just a little bit on a shirt or on your socks, so that when you are feeling sad or lonely you can look down and see a reminder that you are royalty!

 Remember that all girls are princesses, even the mean ones. Have compassion for the girls who want to be in control or treat you badly. Pray for them. Remember they have some sort of "issue" that makes them feel insecure. Jesus asks you to pray for those who persecute you.

 Offer it up. Do you know what that means? It means you take your suffering, humiliation, or bad times and place it at the foot of the cross. Give it to Jesus. This does two things. First, it tells yourself, "I'm in charge of how I feel and how I choose to handle this situation and I am not going to feel sorry for myself and I am not a victim!" Secondly, you are giving a beautiful present to Jesus. This present becomes a prayer that you can say for anyone or anything. For example you can offer it up for the souls in purgatory or for your sick neighbor. Jesus wants you to be happy and joyful but also wants to help you understand that joining your suffering with His can be a good thing.

Stand up for yourself. Learn to let the mean girl know you don't care what she thinks of you. Try comebacks like: "Ya, uh huh. Ok, right...", "Like I care," "Whatever...", "I would care what you think because?" If you don't like what a "friend" says to you, say things like, "That really hurt my feelings." "Don't do that again." "Stop it." If the girl is really mean she probably won't stop bothering you immediately and she'll most likely laugh and say something nasty, but, she'll get the hint that you don't see yourself as the victim and neither should she! This may sound stupid but practice your comebacks so that when you need them you won't be tongue-tied.

Have more than just one group of friends. There's neighborhood kids, friends of family kids, church kids, sports team kids, and so on. Diversify!

There are some great girl saints that have faced worse than the mean girl, like St. Joan of Arc who was completely abandoned by her friends and burnt at the stake as a heretic. Read the lives of the saints to see how they managed. They are entertaining and inspiring.

Forgive that mean girl and don't hold a grudge. That only hurts you.

You Think I'm Mean?

Yes, you could be Loose Lipped Lisa, Jenedict Arnold or any of our other not so nice "friends." All people have the leftovers of original sin that make it easy to be mean. Admit that yes, there have been times when you, yes, *you*! have been unkind. Here's what you can do to change. Just take one step at a time, though, so you don't get overwhelmed

Go to confession and start over.

Ask a close friend for her honest opinion and see if she thinks you're mean. If she is a good friend she will tell you the truth. Make up a secret sign she can give you if you start teasing, gossiping, or any other bad habit you have. Chances are, if you are used to doing these things, you don't even realize you're doing them. Use the signal as a way to stop.

Ask yourself how you would feel if someone gossiped or spread rumors about you. I bet you wouldn't trade places with the victim in a million years.

You, too, can benefit from prayer. Make a specific time each day to pray. Start with something easy like a Hail Mary and get in the habit of praying that same prayer at the same time every day. Any time you want you can talk to Jesus. He's always there to hear your silent prayers. Ask him to help you change and really make an effort. Ask your mom and dad to pray for you, too. They are your advocates and want you to be the best you can be for God!

Remember, girls that are mean probably have issues. What's bothering you? Is it anything that you have control over? Talk to your mom or another trusted adult like an aunt, or counselor. This sounds simple but in today's world many girls have complicated problems that don't go away that easily. It is important to deal with stuff that is bothering you and to get the help you need. Don't underestimate the power of prayer.

You are the daughter of the King.
God loves you sooooo much and has a special plan
for your life. Remember that!

Tools of Meanness

Girls use many "tools" in being mean. There's rumors, the silent treatment, pouting and then there's fashion.

I'm Snooty Susie

I love clothes and love to go shopping. My mom does, too, so we go to the mall at least once a week. Every time I go with mom she buys me whatever I want. I will only shop at Ambercrombie, Hollister, or American Eagle. If I get a gift from a friend or relative that's not from any of those stores, I take it back and go use the money at one of my stores. I wouldn't be caught dead in something from Target. No Way! My friends all wear the same things as me or they're out of the group. one of the things we do for fun at lunch is to point out Walmart or Target outfits on other girls and laugh. Of course we're not mean or anything; they don't even notice, I'm sure. It's always fun to see what Sarah or Katie wear to school. I don't know how they can hold their heads up in public the way they dress. They're both in my homeroom so I get the first look at them. By lunchtime we're all talking and laughing about them. I've never really had them in any of my activities or classes so I don't know them very well. All I know is they are not in my world and I wouldn't want to be seen with them anywhere. I go to church and everything. I see it as another opportunity to see what everyone's wearing and to show off a new outfit. Once a month we have donuts afterwards so I can see my friends. Going to church makes me feel like I'm a good person.

Hi, I'm Sarah

I love school and learning new things. (Sniff) My favorite thing to do is read. I just finished a book on bugs and it was fascinating. I highly recommend it. (Slurp) Oh yes, I'm supposed to tell you about fashion. I find it all such a bore. My grandma usually buys all my clothing from garage sales. I got a lot of things after the church rummage sale. Grandma helped with it and she brought me everything that didn't sell.

Most of the time things don't match (slurp), and don't fit me, but that's ok, I can roll them up or have my mom hem them. I know Susie and her group make fun of me. Somehow, I try to ignore them. If I am concentrating on a book I usually don't even know they exist. Still, it can be hard sometimes in class when we have to work in groups on projects and I am put with her or one of her friends. I don't like being called names (sniff) and I do cry at night sometimes when no one can hear me. I pray to Our Lady for her help. Somehow she always makes me feel better. I have a couple of friends, Olivia and Katie. They get made fun of too. We always stand up for each other and stick together. On the weekends we like to do things outside, watch birds, draw, or discuss our favorite books. I really don't hold (slurp) anything against Susie and her friends. My mom told me that Susie's parents are getting divorced and she has to decide which parent to live with. Mom says that may be why she is so mean. She just wants to make someone else as miserable as she is. Well, as long as I have my own friends I don't care what Susie thinks. My mom always says I should try to pray for Susie but that is hard for me to do. So I just say, "Lord, here's Susie!"

Hey, I'm Olivia

I'm sorry I'm wearing my grass-stained jeans. I was just finishing a game of football with the neighborhood kids. Besides, it would've been hard to find anything clean. All my clothes are under my bed or in my laundry basket. That reminds me, I better throw it all down the chute so mom can wash it, I have been wearing the same pair of undies for 3 days, but don't tell anyone. My mom always told me to have on clean underwear in case I get in an accident and have to go to the hospital. I never did get that. What does underwear have to do with going to the hospital? Well, anyway, I didn't have any clean so I just turned them inside out. I was supposed to ride with you this morning but my mom made me take a shower and wash my hair instead.

I didn't need it washed but she said two weeks was long enough and to get going. You know, I have been so busy hanging outside and getting into different ball games with kids in the neighborhood I have been too busy to do the things mom always bugs me about. She's really bugging me to wear deodorant, wash my face, and especially brush my teeth. After my last visit to the dentist with 5 cavities she has been on my back. I can't believe the dentist wants me to brush twice a day. I'd think once a week would be good. Oh, ya, I'm supposed to be talking about clothes. I just wear what my mom buys for me. I don't worry much about things like that. I just want to get my homework done and go do stuff outside. Sarah and Katie have told me that Susie and her friends laugh at me about how I look. I could care less. I have better things to do than to worry about them; don't you think?

Hi, I'm Katie

I really like fashion and shopping. I try to keep up on the latest stuff through magazines and TV shows. I always like to go to the mall and go to Abercrombie, Hollister and American Eagle to check things out. The only thing is, my family can't afford those places. Mom takes me to Walmart, Target or Shopko. They always have clothes kinda like the expensive stores, but ya know, it's just not the same. There's a group of girls at school that laugh at me and make fun of what I wear. It's just so mean that they say things just because I can't afford to wear the right name brand clothes. I just dread homeroom and lunch. Lately, Sarah and Olivia have been really sticking up for me, and themselves. My mom also told me that these are good things to offer up to Jesus. I hate it when she says stuff like that. I just want all the teasing to go away but she says I shouldn't waste it. Mom says it could help a soul in purgatory or even my own soul. Mom's always good at making me see things differently. She also told me a story about a saint named Margaret. Even her own parents didn't like her because she was deformed. All her life hardly anyone would be her friend, even when she became a sister no one liked her. That makes me think that I can do what Mom says and offer it up. It's not so bad.

Tools of Kindness

Girls use many "tools" for being kind. There's prayers, compassion, understanding, and then there's extending oneself to others. Use your tools today and be kind to someone who needs it!

Fashion Character Quiz

Take this quiz to find out if you are most like Snooty Susie, Studious Sarah, Oblivious Olivia, or Cute Katie. Tally your answers at the end.

1. On a trip to the mall I would be able to buy:
   a. A t-shirt and jeans from Abercrombie.
   b. A book on my favorite subject.
   c. I don't really like going to the mall.
   d. An outfit on sale from a discount or second hand store

2. The three things I do to take care of myself everyday are:
   a. I have more than three things I do. Here's a few: Mary Kay skincare program, shower, blow dry my hair, apply lip gloss and powder, use my deodorant, brush my teeth, dress in my name brand clothing only, spritz on my designer perfume.
   b. I shower and shampoo my hair and brush my teeth.
   c. I always get up late and am rushing out the door. I'm lucky to get my teeth brushed.
   d. I shower and shampoo my hair, cleanse my face with soap and water, brush my teeth and dress as nice as I can for the day.

3. How often do I make fun of, laugh at, tease, or ignore other girls?
   a. I'm not mean or anything, but I do often all of the above.
   b. I don't really have time to notice things going on with other girls. I have my studies to keep me busy.
   c. I have been known to say a mean thing here or there to someone who makes fun of me. Most of the time I don't care because I like to be with my friends and do our own thing.
   d. Usually I am the one people make fun of since I don't wear name brand clothing.

4. What are the things I think about most?
   a. How I dress, how many friends I have, what boy I have a crush on.
   b. My schoolwork and being with my friends.
   c. Having fun and playing sports.
   d. Getting along with the popular girls and trying to fit in.

5. How much time a day do I spend saying my prayers or thinking about Jesus?

    a. I hardly ever think about God unless I go to church.
    b. I pray at mealtime with my family and before I go to bed.
    c. I pray when my mom or dad reminds me. It's not that I don't love Jesus, I just forget about him.
    d. I pray a lot and ask Jesus to help me during the day so I can get through the teasing and laughing.

Key

At least 4 a's: You are most like Snooty Susie. It's a good idea to put yourself in the other girl's spot and think about how she feels. Ask yourself, "How would I feel if girls were making fun of me or laughing at me?" You may have to go to confession if you have made a habit of being the mean girl. Praying and talking to Our Lady and Jesus will help you turn from the cruel chick into a happy girl with lots of friends.

At least 4 b's: You are most like Studious Sarah. You know what's important to you and you don't worry too much about what the mean chicks think. Continue to stand up for yourself and spend time praying everyday.

At least 4 c's: You are most like Oblivious Olivia. You have a lot of good things going. You are a good friend and like to have fun. It's a good idea to start taking better care of your body. You are growing up and are not a little girl anymore. Have your mom help you get into the habit of brushing your teeth everyday, and a schedule for showers. You may want to start using a skincare program. It's good that you don't care about what others think of you, but it's not good that you don't take care of yourself. Keep up your prayers.

At least 4 d's You are most like Cute Katie. You take care of yourself and like to be in fashion. You need to realize how special you are and that what brands of clothing you wear do not make you who your are. It is good that you are learning to offer up your hurt feelings to Jesus. He will help you. Pray that you can love yourself the way He does so that what the mean chicks say and do won't bother you. You have good friends to have fun with so hang with them.

THAT'S SOOOOO MEAN...

Molly and Mindy were friends and rode the school bus together every day. Mindy was the first to get on every morning so she would save a spot for Molly. One day Mindy didn't feel like saving a seat and let another girl sit in Molly's place. When Molly got on the bus looking for a place to sit, Mindy replied, "How was I supposed to know your mom wasn't going to take you today?" Molly ended up sitting in the back with the rowdy boys wondering why her friend would do that.

Rachel, Rita and Riley were in the same grade. They hung around each other but had various friends. One day, Rachel called Rita to see if she wanted to play an "innocent trick" on Riley. Rachel explained that she had three way calling and could call Riley at the same time. Rachel would then set her up by getting her to say things about Rita not knowing that Rita was listening. "Wouldn't it be fun to see what she really thinks of you?" asked Rachel. Rita agreed. She wasn't expecting to be so hurt about the things said about her. The next day she confronted Riley, who was totally embarrassed. Eventually, Riley and Rita made up and ditched Rachel.

Laura was telling Lindsey that she thought Danny was the cutest! After all, they were best buds and Laura knew Lindsey would never tell a soul. The next day at school someone had put papers all over Danny's locker with "Laura loves Danny" and "Laura wants to kiss Danny." Danny was grossed out and Laura spent days crying over the whole trauma. She was smart enough to never trust Lindsey again.

Allison and Annie hung around together all the time. For the most part, the girls got along great. After a while, though, Allison would always insist on having her way. Annie, being an easygoing soul, would give in to Allison's demands. One day she Annie really wanted to watch her favorite movie but Allison wanted something else. Annie stood her ground. Allison gave her the silent treatment for a week. After a few more "silent treatments," Annie wisely decided to let that "friendship" go.

Bella liked to call the shots. She had great ideas that all the girls in the group went along with. Bella planned a super sleepover with takeout, movies, and crafts. Everyone in the group was invited, that is, everyone but Blair. Eventually word got around and everyone was buzzing about the big event. Blair realized she wasn't invited and asked a "trusted" friend what the deal was. She replied, "Well, we're all going. Too bad for you." Blair went home and bawled her eyes out the entire weekend.

ALWAYS REMEMBER
THE GOLDEN RULE!

DO TO OTHERS WHATEVER YOU
WOULD HAVE THEM DO TO YOU.
MATTHEW 7:12

Cyber Meanness

Take it from me girls; I have seen my share of meanness. Not only have I heard about some very sad stories involving uncharitable acts of jealousy or vengeance during my many years as a TV and radio news reporter and Catholic talk show host, but I also experienced meanness firsthand when I was your age. I was teased and made fun of by the very people I thought cared about me; girls I called "friends."

Today, friends talk to each other in all sorts of unique ways. You can converse face to face at school, or during a gathering at someone's home, or maybe at the local mall. Thanks to all the neat advances in technology, most of you also probably keep in touch in a variety of other ways as well. As long as mom and dad approve, and are supervising, it's also nice to occasionally communicate over the phone or keep in touch through the Internet via e-mail or instant messaging. Communicating with your close friends is an important part of life. The Lord wants us to have good friends who share in our ups and downs and laugh and cry with us. The Bible tells us in the Old Testament Book of Proverbs Chapter 17 vs17 that *"a friend loves at all times."*

But what happens when those friends that are supposed to love us, don't show love and instead turn on us? Well, it hurts. It can hurt more than we are able to imagine. In my case, the girls whom I thought were my friends kicked me out of the school locker we shared and threw my belongings all over the school floor; all because I wouldn't do something with them that deep down I knew was wrong. They called me names such as "teacher's pet" and "goodie two shoes." Maybe these names seem lame to you or you recognize how hurtfully they were flung at me, either way, I was devastated. After all, these were my "friends!" Somehow I found strength in my Catholic faith and I made myself move on to a new locker and eventually new friends.

Here's the big difference between then and now; since we didn't have communications tools such as the Internet, cell phones, e-mail, instant messaging, chat rooms, and social gathering sites on the web, my story was quickly old news.

Unfortunately that's often not the case today. If you say something mean to or about someone on the Internet, or if someone says something about you, not only could your entire school know about it in a matter of minutes, but so could the entire community or even the country! That's why it is important to always remember that everyone you know and everyone you don't know are all sons and daughters of the King. Everyone you meet is unique and has great dignity and must be treated with love and respect by following the King's Golden Rule; *"In everything herefore, treat people the same way you want them to treat you, for this is he Law and the Prophets."* Ladies it's pretty simple isn't it? If you want o be treated nicely, be nice. Even if this seems impossible, find strength n your faith. God is there for you even when your friends aren't!

Sometimes though, our anger, tempers, or the frustrations of someone else can take over and a person loses control and acts wrongly toward another. "Mean girl" stories are on the news and tell about bullying or fighting that has been posted on the Internet for the entire world to see. So while it's great to have friends, it's important to take your methods of communicating with those friends seriously in order to avoid something as tragic as cyber bullying or cyber meanness.

What is cyber bullying? Well, according to www.stopcyberbullying.org, "cyberbullying" or "cyber meanness" is *"when a child, preteen or teen is teased, tormented, humiliated, embarrassed or targeted by another child, preteen, or teen using the internet or other interactive technical devices."* Cyberbullying usually involves frequent communication through one of the technical devices we've already mentioned and according to police, if the cyberbullying is strong enough it could result in the young person doing the bullying facing some serious charges. Cyberbullying can occur in a number of different ways. Sometimes one person targets another. For example, if I was growing up right now in the 21st century my friends may have chosen to call me names in writing through e-mail or text message, instead of bullying me in person. The contact could have easily resulted in a case of what we would call today "cyber bullying" or meanness. Or the cyber-bullies can hide behind another person and have them send messages or do the bullying for them. Or the cyber-bullies can pretend they are someone else and do send their own hateful and hurtful messages. You get the picture, and it isn't pretty nor is it appropriate behavior for you, the beautiful princess, a daughter of the King.

So what can and should you do about this common problem of cyber bullying? Well, since Jesus tells us in the Gospel of St. Matthew 7:5

that we need to *"remove the plank out of our own eye before pointing to speck in our brother's eye,"* that means we have to do an examination of conscience and see if we might have acted inappropriately by being a cyber-meanie ourselves.

Take a look at how you have treated your friends or school mates recently. Sit down with your mom or dad and if you have been allowed to use e mail or instant messaging, talk about and review the messages you have sent. Take an **honest** look at the language that was used and apply the Golden Rule. Can you say the language in the messages or communication was kind and polite? Or did they include name calling and insults? Think about how you would feel if those same messages were directed at you? If you did act inappropriately, ask Jesus for forgiveness and then apologize for your actions. If you are old enough to go to receive the Sacrament of Reconciliation, go to Jesus in Confession and tell the Priest you are sorry for your sins. Then try your very best every day to remember that verse in Proverbs which calls us to love our friends. And if you feel yourself getting angry and ready to pounce on those computer keys again, step back take a breath and most importantly say a prayer until you are calm and can write a Christ-like note.

What should you do if you are one being bullied? Don't be afraid to tell. As we just mentioned some of the cases of cyberbullying have had disastrous results that have made headlines. Your parents care. Your teachers care and if you care about doing the right thing, you will, in the long run, be helping the person who is acting wrongly. You may not feel it now but telling on someone who is cyber-bullying is the right thing to do. So if you feel you are being threatened, or if cyber meanness has been occurring frequently, it's important to follow through and let adults know so they can address the situation. Remember that if someone is hurting you, they are not your friend. I found new friends and you will, too. You are a daughter of the King and deserve to be treated with respect and dignity.

Finally, there are some really good web sites that can help you, your friends, classmates, and family address this important issue of meanness. Why not be the one to raise awareness at school, in your neighborhood, and at home? Talk to your parents and teachers about learning more from such sites as www.cyberbullying.org, www.netsmartz.org, and www.netsmartzkids.org which can help you and other young people get smart when it comes to all of those technical gizmos and gadgets. Technology is not a bad thing, as long as we used it correctly and no one gets hurt in the process. Friendship and being a daughter of the King is all about loving all of God's creatures, especially His most precious creatures; you and me.

"A new command I give you; Love one another as I
have loved you, so you must love one another. By all
this men will know that you are my disciples."
John 13:34-35

A Bit About Boys

"Boys are made of snips and snails and puppy dog tails." Ooooo, yuck! Somewhere in the near future, if not now, boys will go from being gross to something interesting, and well, cute. Yes, it's true; boys have crushes on girls and girls have crushes on boys. This is all natural as you grow from a little girl into a young woman. However, there are some basic facts to know as a daughter of the King.

Boys think way different than girls. They have no idea why you cry, laugh hysterically, or get upset. Don't hold it against them: that's just the way they're wired. They just don't get "it."

Boys grow up slower than girls so when you're ready to have a rational conversation, they're still playing with Legos and making grunting noises.

Boys need to respect girls and treat them like they would Our Lady. Girls, ***do not settle for less!*** You're a daughter of the King and deserve to be treated like royalty. If you don't expect it, you won't get it.

Boys should never, never, never push, hit, kick, punch, or wrestle with a girl. This is huge! Many women that end up in front of the annulment tribunal were slapped or hit by their spouse even before they were married. Any time a boy is rough with you, run like the wind! (and tell on him). Remember this is no way to treat a princess.

When the time comes for you to court, or date, (and this is up to your parents to let you know when you are ready), never, never, never, chase, call, email, IM, or text the boy first. Yes this sounds very old fashioned but this is basic for the daughter of the King. In this day and age boys are so confused about how to be a young man because girls have taken over. In days of old, back when there were knights and beautiful ladies, the knights would perform acts of kindness and heroism to win the lady's heart.

Boys...

When the lady decided his affection for her was sincere, then she would allow him to pursue her, with her parents' permission of course. You daughters of the King deserve this as well. Do not give your heart away too easily or quickly, even if it's just a crush in 6th grade. Don't let him have your friendship without a little work on his part.

Boys and girls your age should be friends. It is good to socialize with boys at school, church, or a family activity where you can talk, play games, or hangout. "Going with" and "having a boyfriend" just means you like a boy. Where do you really get to go? If you start going places alone, or having boy-girl parties what will there be to look forward to when you get in high school? So many girls today are in such a hurry to "grow up." Just take things one day at a time and enjoy things like reading, girl time, shopping, sports, and hobbies. Don't let boys take over everything you and your friends think about. Dating or courting should be saved until you are ready to find a husband. In the meantime, do things in groups and with families. A lot of grown ups talk about the "good old days" of innocence because those days were good! You are innocent and these are your good old days, right here, right now! You are creating memories by the way you live at this very moment in time. When you have fun with your friends and do things as a daughter of the King, you are making memories that you will look back upon as the "good old days." Make memories you will cherish and look back on with happiness.

Pay attention to all the things boys do now. Watch how they treat their mothers and sisters. When there's someone who gets picked on, check out how a boy reacts. Those who stand up for the underdog have kind hearts. Put this data in the back of your mind and pull it out when you're old enough to be looking for a husband, if that is your vocation. Again, remember, you are the daughter of the King. Don't settle for less than a son of the King, a prince.

Boys are different than girls. That's what makes them so interesting. So, now you know some things about boys. Go have some fun with the girls!

Things to Think About

An examination of conscience for girls.

- Do I make fun of or tease other girls?
- Do I gossip or tell stories about girls that aren't true?
- Do I tell secrets to others?
- Do I judge girls by what kind of clothes they wear?
- Do I wear things that are not modest?
- Have I ever left a girl out because of how she looks?
- Have I ever told other girls not to include someone?
- Do I call names?
- Do I pout if I don't get my way?
- Have I ever refused to talk to a friend if she doesn't do what I want?
- Do I forget to brush my teeth, shower or wash my hair because I am lazy?
- Am I boy crazy?
- Do I call, email, text or IM boys?

A long time ago a very wise bishop told his people that the goodness of the world follows the goodness of the girls. Wow! Girls have great power.

Virtues to Live By

What is a virtue? Very simply, a virtue is a good habit that inclines you to do whatever is good. Virtuous behavior helps us live good, happy lives. But there is more to virtues than that. A single good action does not constitute a virtue. For instance, a person wouldn't be considered to have the virtue of generosity if she shared her candy with her friends only once. In order to become a virtue, a good habit has to be repeated on a regular basis.

Loyalty and Friendship

Loyalty is having a bond to people, faith and country. The habit of living this out includes standing up for your friends. When someone says bad things about a friend in front of you, it is the virtue of loyalty that makes you stand up for her and kindly stop the criticism. If this doesn't work you simply walk away, taking your pal with you.

If you are loyal, you truly care about your friend and never do anything to hurt her. You help her through tough times, or visit her when she is sick. You always tell the truth, even if it is unpleasant and you keep your friend's secrets.

Talking bad about her behind her back, gossiping or lying are ways of betraying your friend, which is lack of loyalty. Remember, Jesus was betrayed by one of his closest friends, Judas.

Here are some possible goals to help you be a loyal friend:
Speak kindly of everyone
Stand up for your friend
if others are mean to her or are teasing her
Keep rumors to yourself
Always think the best of people
Keep your promises to your friends

A Girl Like Me

St. Bernadette

Bernadette Soubirous was born in Lourdes, France in the year 1844. Her father and mother were strong Catholics and had five children. Her father was a good-natured man, but was not a not a good provider for his family because he struggled with alcoholism. Her mother was forced to take odd jobs to help feed the family. Many times Bernadette and her brothers and sisters went to bed with their stomachs growling from hunger. The Soubirous family lived in a small one-room building that had once been a jail.

Bernadette was a good-natured girl but was known for being strong willed. She struggled in school and was considered "slow." She suffered from asthma, which kept her home on many occasions, making school even harder for her. Bernadette had not made her First Communion even though she was fourteen years old because she did not know her religion well enough.

One day in February, Bernadette, her sister, and their friend Joan went to a wooded area called Massabielle to gather firewood. There was a stream on the way that the girls had to cross. Mary and Joan quickly removed their shoes and stockings and hurried across to the other side. Bernadette hesitated while the two girls ran ahead. Suddenly, Bernadette felt a breeze and saw the branches of some trees near a small rocky area called a grotto, move. A beautiful young Lady appeared. Instantly, Bernadette dropped to her knees and accustomed to praying the rosary, pulled out her beads and began reciting. The Lady also had a rosary and followed on her beads, joining her with the Glory Be prayer. After the rosary was completed the Lady disappeared.

Bernadette told Mary and Joan what she had seen. They were so excited they told their parents and friends, who all thought it was nonsense. The next week Bernadette wanted to return to where she had seen the vision. Her father gave her a little bottle of holy water to take with her and her friends to the grotto. They knelt to pray the rosary and as Bernadette looked upward, the Lady appeared, seen only by Bernadette. Bernadette took the holy water and threw it at the vision, making sure the Lady was from God.

Word spread of Bernadette's visions to the authorities who did not believe her. The police commissioner questioned Bernadette and suspected the ordeal to be a scam to get money. They harassed Bernadette but she stood up to their ridicule, always telling the truth. The townspeople were curious and many mocked her. She returned to the grotto with people curious to see what was happening. This time the Lady spoke. She asked Bernadette to return 15 times, which she happily agreed to do. During this time, the pastor of the parish and other religious did not believe her. They wanted Bernadette to find out the name of the Lady. The Lady replied, "I am the Immaculate Conception." Only four years earlier, the Pope had officially taught that Mary was conceived without sin, which means that Mary is "The Immaculate Conception." The apparition was truly Mary the Mother of God! Soon the pastor and church authorities approved the visions.

During the remaining apparitions Our Lady asked Bernadette to have a chapel built where the appearances were occurring. She also asked Bernadette to, "Go and drink and wash yourself in the spring. Then eat some of the grass you will find there." There was no spring! The Lady pointed, and Bernadette began to dig in the sand, which filled up with water. Bernadette cupped her hand, drank and washed her face, then ate the bitter grass growing there. The crowd of people looking on were astonished and laughed at her. The Lady told Bernadette that Bernadette couldn't be promised happiness in this life but in the next. As the days went by, the little hole became a stream. Today, it flows into large tanks where people go to bathe. Over the years many have been cured of illnesses and other conditions.

Bernadette hated all the attention the people gave her because of the visions. She went to the convent where she felt she was unworthy to be a sister and only asked to be a maid. The Mother General received her into the convent happily and Bernadette took her vows. Many of the nuns treated her harshly and were jealous of her.

Bernadette worked in the kitchen and embroidered vestments for priests. She developed tuberculosis, which caused her much pain. Remembering Our Lady's promise for happiness, Bernadette died at the age of 35.

You've Gotta Have A Plan!

You know it is important to take care of and control your body. In the same way, you need to take care of your soul. You need to nourish it so that it can grow in friendship with Jesus. How is that done? You gotta have a plan! Do you think athletes make it to the Olympics by chance? Do you think they go with the flow and train here and there and somehow one day they end up in the Olympic games winning a medal? Of course not, you know that! They have a plan that includes diet and training. They follow it everyday, even when they don't feel like it. This dedication allows the athlete to attain their goal, their dream of winning a medal at the Olympics. Think about the purpose of your life: to know, love and serve God in this life and to be happy with Him forever in the next. Do you think you can achieve this goal without some planning and preparation? Here's a simple but effective plan you can use your entire life to complete your training here and attain your Heavenly goal.

What things should be part of your plan?

Morning offering:

A good way to start your day is to say, "Hello, Jesus!" The day ahead is a great gift from God. The morning offering consists of giving Jesus everything you will do and say that day. Tell Him you want to please Him and give Him glory in all that you do. You can make up your own special prayer or you can choose one to memorize. For example, here's a very simple prayer. *"Good Morning dear Jesus this day is for you, I ask you to bless all that I say and do. Amen"* or *"Oh Jesus through the Immaculate Heart of Mary I offer you the prayers, works, joys, and sufferings of this day, For all the intentions of Your Sacred Heart, in union with the Holy Sacrifice of the Mass said throughout the world today, in reparation for my sins, for the intentions of all our associates, and for the intentions of the Holy Father this month. Amen"* It is important to try and say your morning offering at the same time every day so that you remember to do it. Some girls will say it right when they wake up. Others, when they sit down to breakfast. Whatever works for you, just do it!

Daily Prayer:

Prayer is talking to Jesus. It is something great! Jesus prayed and openly encouraged his disciples to pray. And guess what? You, as a daughter of the King, are a disciple. How does a person learn to pray? Start out by setting aside 5 minutes of your day to sit down in a quiet place where there will be no distractions. Place yourself in the presence of Jesus, asking your guardian angel to help you start a conversation with Jesus. Because prayer is an intimate conversation with God, you can talk to God as your best friend and tell Him the things that are concerning you, what is making you happy, angry or sad; God is always listening.

You may tell him something like: *"Hi Jesus, guess what I'm doing today? I'm going to my cousins' house! Mom said I have to clean my room before going....and you know Jesus, I hate cleaning my room! But I guess I'll do it.... Maybe I should offer it up for a special intention, eh? Who needs prayers, Jesus?....."* *On you go.* You are praying! Slowly increase the 5 minutes of prayer a day to 10 minutes. You will feel so happy when you spend time talking to Jesus every day!

The Rosary of the Blessed Mother

Do you enjoy looking at family pictures and remembering those precious moments? Well, when you pray the rosary you contemplate moments in the lives of Jesus and Mary on each mystery. The rosary is divided into 4 parts: each part into five mysteries. For each mystery one Our Father and Ten Hail Mary's are prayed while you meditate on a certain time of Jesus' life. The name rosary means "crown of roses". Think about each of the Hail Mary's you pray as a rose offered to Our Lady. By the end of the rosary, you have offered her a huge bouquet of beautiful roses! If saying the entire rosary seems like a big task, start out with just one decade and slowly add one at a time. The idea is to make the effort and to keep on trying.

Examination of conscience at night.

Before going to bed, it's a good idea to take a quick look at your day in God's presence to see if you have behaved as a daughter of the King. An easy way to do this is by asking yourself these three questions:

> 1) *What did I do today that was pleasing to God?*
> 2) *What did I do today that was not pleasing to God?*
> 3) *What does God want me to do better tomorrow?*

Ponder briefly on each question, and then follow with an act of contrition to tell Jesus that you are sorry for having offended Him. An Act of Contrition is just a short prayer telling Jesus you are sorry for your sins. It can be as simple as *"I'm sorry, Lord. Help me do better tomorrow."* Or it can be the traditional Act of Contrition, *"Oh my God, I am heartily sorry for having offended thee and I detest all my sins because of the loss of Heaven and the pains of Hell, But most of all because they offend Thee my God who are all good and deserving of all my love. I firmly resolve with the help of Thy grace, to confess my sins, to do penance and to amend my life, Amen."*

Pray three Hail Mary's at night

Before going to bed, ask the Blessed Mother to help you keep your heart pure.

Don't delay, start today,
you can win the Olympics of the spiritual life.
Order your special All Things Girl journal today!

Printed in the United States
128910LV00001B